The JOY of Adolescent Catechesis

MW01671143

NIAC
The National Initiative on Adolescent Catechesis

Publication of the Partnership on Adolescent Catechesis

NATIONAL CONFERENCE FOR CATECHETICAL LEADERSHIP

NFCYM
NATIONAL FEDERATION FOR CATHOLIC YOUTH MINISTRY

NCEA®
National Catholic Educational Association

Copyright ©2017 National Federation for Catholic Youth Ministry, the National Catholic Educational Association and the National Conference for Catechetical Leadership (Partnership on Adolescent Catechesis). All rights reserved, including the right to reproduce in whole or in part in any form without the written permission of the copyright holders. Permission may be sought from any of the copyright holders.
Second Printing 2017

NFCYM
415 Michigan Avenue, N.E., Suite 40
Washington, D.C. 20017
202.636.3825
www.nfcym.org

NCEA
1005 N. Glebe Rd., Suite 525
Arlington, VA 22201
571.257.0010
www.NCEA.org

NCCL
415 Michigan Avenue, N.E., Suite 200
Washington, D.C. 20017
202.884.9753
www.nccl.org

ISBN: 978-1-55833-619-3
Part Number: REL-60-1566

Table of Contents

Acknowledgements

This document would not have been possible without the commitment and passion of numerous people. It is the result of a long process of exploration, study, and discussion. The Partnership for Adolescent Catechesis would like to acknowledge the work of the following people and groups:

Writing Team:

Bob Rice, Ph.D – primary author

Miriam Hidalgo – primary author

Elzbieta Milewska

William Miller

Nannette Coons

Peter Ductram

Craig Gould

Vincent Guider

Christopher Miller

Mark Pacione†

Partnership for Adolescent Catechesis Representatives (Past and Present):

*Indicates a past or organizational representative.

From NFCYM: Michael Theisen
Robert McCarty, D.Min.
*D. Scott Miller

From NCEA: Andrea Kopp
*Mickie Abatemarco
*Lori Dahlhoff, Ed.D.
*Christopher Cosentino
*Rev. John Serio, SDB
*Diana Dudoit Raiche, Ph.D.
*Gary Meyerl
*Robert Colbert
*Chris Scalise

From NCCL: Margaret Matijasevic
William Miller
*Harry Dudley
*Leland Nagel†
*Mark Pacione†
*Neil Parent

From NIAC: Elzbieta Milewska

With Support from the Staff and Offices of the United States Conference of Catholic Bishops:

Evangelization and Catechesis: Jeannine Marino, JCL
*Fr. Brian Bransfield
*Daniel S. Mulhall

Laity, Marriage, Family Life, and Youth: Paul Jarzembowski
*Sr. Eileen McCann, CSJ

Cultural Diversity in the Church: Alejandro Aguilera-Titus

†Leland Nagel and Mark Pacione both died unexpectedly during the process of developing this document. Lee and Mark were passionate life-long advocates for transformative catechesis that draws families, children, youth, and adults to Christ.

A Letter to Those Who Minister with Young Catholics in the United States

Dear Sisters and Brothers in Christ,

Thank you for saying "yes" to the catechetical mission of helping young people grow in their relationship with the Lord, and thus become more passionate and dedicated disciples! For two thousand years, the Church has flourished from generation to generation because of people like you who are willing to take the time to share with others the faith and love you have for Jesus Christ.

We are the Partnership for Adolescent Catechesis (PAC). Formed in 2003, the PAC is a unique collaboration of the National Federation for Catholic Youth Ministry, the National Catholic Educational Association, and the National Conference for Catechetical Leadership, with support from the United States Conference of Catholic Bishops; in particular the Secretariats of Cultural Diversity in the Church; Evangelization and Catechesis; and Laity, Marriage, Family Life, and Youth.

The passion we have for our faith leads us to intentionally form other disciples through a fruitful catechesis and formation in the life of the Church. We have written this document to inspire and challenge all who participate in this joyful and at times demanding ministry of adolescent catechesis.

This ministry gives us the opportunity to invite young people to have a personal and intimate relationship with Jesus Christ through the Catholic Church. It is just one stage in a lifelong process of faith formation, but an important one. Moreover, it strives to form young disciples by empowering them to know, love, and serve Christ in every personal encounter in their daily lives.

The reality of catechesis is that it is more than instruction in the faith. St. John Paul II emphasized this point when he said that "an intellectual knowledge of Christ and his Gospel is not enough."[1]

[1]St. John Paul II, "Jubilee of Catechists and Religion Teachers," (Homily, Vatican City, December 10, 2000).

Although it is important to learn about our faith, our mission is not just to inform but to form and transform. Jesus is not a subject to study but a person to encounter. Though this mission is challenging, we are inspired by our love for young people and the hope we see in their eyes. Pope Francis has written:

> Every form of catechesis should attend to the 'way of beauty'... Proclaiming Christ means showing that to believe in and to follow him is not only something right and true, but also something beautiful, capable of filling life with new splendor and profound joy, even in the midst of difficulties.[2]

We make a profound difference in the lives of teenagers by sharing with them, in words and deeds, the beauty of the Catholic faith. Our young people not only desperately need to see and hear what it means to be Catholic; they need to be apprenticed into the faith.

Be Not Afraid! Be Excited!

All of us are on a journey of continual conversion. Pope Francis often speaks of having an encounter with Jesus – a personal, intimate relationship that allows Christ to enter into our lives and transform us from within. In the process, we are touched by God's grace and changed forever for the better.

Do not be afraid! God has chosen us to accompany young people on their journey of faith! Sometimes the work may feel overwhelming, but here lies the beauty of grace. Grace empowers us to be witnesses of faith, and the grace of the Holy Spirit works in the lives of young people to invite them to conversion. We may never see the results of ministry with young people, because often we are seed planters but not harvesters, joining a chorus of others who have planted or will plant the seeds of faith and love in the lives of our young people. And, as we are reminded by St. Paul, the harvest comes in due season.[3]

One of the wonderful things about participating in this ministry is that it gives us a chance to grow in our own Catholic identity. Just as our young people are called, we too are called to

[2]Pope Francis, *Evangelii Gaudium* (Vatican City: Libreria Editrice Vaticana, 2013), no. 167.
[3]Galatians 6:9.

seek Christ through the beautiful lens of our Catholic faith. By developing habits of daily prayer, reading sacred Scripture, participating in the sacraments and spending time in loving service to others, we grow in our relationship with the Lord. Moreover, as we model these practices for those we catechize, we are mentoring them in the faith.

Conversion is a work of the Holy Spirit. It is the work of divine grace. The Holy Spirit working in us speaks to the Holy Spirit working in youth. We are not using the Spirit to help us accomplish our ministry; we are instruments in the sacred ministry of Christ. We must hold on to this profound truth! There is great peace and joy in knowing that this is God's work, not ours. By the same token, it is important to remember that, though we may play a small role in God's bigger plan for these young people, it is an important one. Teenagers are at a critical point in their development. Our ministry with them during this time may well impact the rest of their lives. Moreover, knowing that this ministry is done through the power of the Holy Spirit should not cause us to be passive. It should encourage us to be passionate and to give God our best. We are privileged to share the love of Christ with others, and to share with them the reason for our faith and our hope in Christ's promises of abundant life.

Our Prayer for the Future

The Church has no shortage of words; what she needs are more witnesses. The Church cries out for more individuals who choose to be missionary disciples, who are willing to accompany young people on their journey of faith and to show them what it means to be disciples of Jesus Christ in the Catholic Church.

Thank you for answering God's call! Let us pray that we will always recognize the presence of the Holy Spirit, guiding us in wisdom and courage as, together, we strive to hand on the faith to the next generation of Catholic teenagers in the United States.

In Christ,

The Partnership for Adolescent Catechesis

The Joy of Adolescent Catechesis

"Good teacher, what must I do to inherit eternal life?"[4]

Jesus responded to this question, posed by an affluent man described in the Bible as "young," with both an affirmation of the commandments and an invitation to discipleship. The young man went away sad because he was unwilling to surrender his current lifestyle in order to follow Jesus. However, in Christ's company there was another young man, the Apostle John, who had renounced everything to follow Jesus. Here we see the contrast. One young man was too attached to his possessions and faded into anonymity. The other committed himself to following Jesus and powerfully changed the world, in Christ's name.

This is the choice the Church offers to young people today. In a world that encourages them to be governed by passions and led by emotions, Christ invites them to the "noble and authentic adventure"[5] of being his disciples. As those who work with teenagers can attest, it is a joy to bring them the Good News and invite them into a deeper relationship with Jesus Christ through the teaching, sacramental life, community, and good works of the Catholic Church.

The Joy of Adolescent Catechesis has been written to inspire those who are involved in catechetical ministry with adolescents. In the process, it strives to expand the vision of passing on a vibrant and joyful faith to teenagers. It is an invitation to examine, thoroughly and honestly, current assumptions and systems in order to encourage the creation of new relationships and patterns of ministry. All of these activities will, by the grace of God, work together to form dedicated disciples for Jesus Christ.[6]

[4] Mark 10:17.

[5] St. John Paul II, 1995 *World Day of Prayer for Vocations*, in *Renewing the Vision: A Framework for Catholic Youth Ministry* (Washington, D.C.: USCCB Publishing, 1997), pg. 10.

[6] *cf.* National Initiative on Adolescent Catechesis, *Vision and Outcomes Statement for the National Initiative on Adolescent Catechesis* (2009), p. 1.

This document does not explore, in depth, specific topics of catechesis; nor is it meant to be a "toolbox" providing specific ways to address young people in particular catechetical settings. It is designed to encourage conversation and collaboration among all who share the goal of providing new, relevant methods for bringing young people to Christ.

The Vision of Adolescent Catechesis

Placing Catechesis in Context

The Church exists to proclaim the Good News of Jesus Christ and to draw his people into a relationship with him. In other words, the Church exists to evangelize.[7] All that she does is intended to further this goal. "Catechesis is an indispensable stage in the rich, complex, dynamic reality of evangelization."[8]

Understanding that catechesis is an integral part of evangelization leads clearly to its outcomes. The documents of the Catholic Church have provided beautiful language to describe the goals of catechesis: "[to] put people not only in touch but in communion, in intimacy, with Jesus Christ,"[9] Succinctly, the goal of catechesis is missionary discipleship. The Catechism of the Catholic Church states: "Quite early on, the name catechesis was given to the totality of the Church's efforts to make disciples, to help men believe that Jesus is the Son of God so that believing they might have life in his name, and to educate and instruct them in this life, thus building up the body of Christ."[10]

The content of adolescent catechesis is Jesus Christ himself. Adolescent catechesis should engage teenagers in an ongoing conversation that will lead them to the realization that God became flesh and dwelt among us as Jesus. Pope Francis beautifully sums up the message of the Gospel, also known as the kerygma, in this way: "Jesus Christ loves you; he gave his life to save you; and now he is living at your side every day to enlighten, strengthen, and free you."[11] He calls this the "first proclamation," not because it is

> *How would you personally sum up the kerygma – the core message of the Gospel - to a young person who asks you what our faith is all about?*
>
> *How central is the proclamation of the kerygma in your ministry?*

[7]Paul VI, *Evangelii Nuntiandi*, (Vatican City: Libreria Editrice Vaticana, 1975), p. 14.
[8]USCCB, National Directory for Catechesis, (Washington, D.C., 2005), pp. 41-42.
[9]St. John Paul II. Catechesi Tradendae, (Vatican City: Libreria Editrice Vaticana, 1979), p. 5.
[10]*Catechism of the Catholic Church* (Vatican City: Libreria Editrice Vaticana, 1993), p. 4.
[11]*Evangelii Gaudium*, p. 164.

something given at the beginning and then done away with, but because it is primary in our catechesis. Everything we say and do in catechesis is centered on this profound truth.

This is accomplished through professing the Creed, celebrating the sacraments, living a moral life in solidarity with all our sisters and brothers in Christ, and learning how to pray, thus becoming leaven for the Kingdom of God in the world. These are the "four pillars" of catechesis, and the mission that Christ has entrusted to us. No matter the topic, the heart of what we proclaim is always an invitation to intimacy with Jesus Christ, who leads us into the life of the Trinity, a life of love, "the love that never ends."[12] Through his death and resurrection, Jesus offers eternal life to those who believe in him.[13] Catechesis should be more than informative; it should lead to personal and pastoral conversion, a life-changing encounter with the living God through the power of the Holy Spirit, to make the world anew.

In critically examining your catechetical program(s), how balanced are they in engaging the three dimensions of head, heart and hands? What can be done to create a more balanced and holistic approach to catechesis?

The term catechesis is often used interchangeably with religious education. For the purpose of this document, religious education is defined as instruction in the beliefs, tenets, and practices of a faith (cognitive). Religious education is always a part of catechesis, but it is not the only part. Catechesis also includes an affective (feelings and emotions) component and a behavioral (how one lives) component. Effective catechesis is not just informative, but transformative of the head, heart, hands, and ultimately the soul of the believer.

Taking this into account, we realize that a significant portion of catechesis occurs well beyond the classroom or formal religious education settings. It begins in the home, within the family. It is profoundly present in all of the liturgical and sacramental experiences of the Faith. It is found in the very fabric of all cultural traditions lived by Christians all over the world. For, as St. John Paul II said at a gathering of Native American leaders in Phoenix, Arizona in 1987, "The Catholic Faith can thrive in any culture." Catechesis also occurs in casual, yet intentional, conversations between believers and during spiritual reflection upon everyday experiences.

[12]*Catechism of the Catholic Church* (Vatican City: Libreria Editrice Vaticana, 1993), 25.
[13]*cf.* John 11:25.

Understanding the Concept of Adolescence

Before catechesis with adolescents can be thoroughly examined, it is important to define what is meant by the word "adolescence" in the context of this document. The term "adolescence" is derived from the Latin "adolesc" which means "to grow." There are a variety of views concerning when it starts and ends, but it is commonly accepted to begin at puberty and end at legal majority.[14] For the purpose of this document "adolescence" and "adolescent" will refer to young people ages 12 to 18, typically situated in grades six through twelve. (Moreover, in the present context, the term "adolescent" is synonymous with the terms "young person" and "teen/teenager.")

The world and the lives of young people are often in flux. The young are easily influenced by the messages and stereotypes that society constantly feeds them. They communicate differently than adults communicate, often leading to misunderstanding and sometimes to conflict. Although still needing the security and guidance of parents and other family members, teens are also trying to assert their independence. It is not a coincidence that the one story we have of Jesus as a young person involves powerful revelation but also miscommunication and anxiety within the family.[15]

What are three of the most influential ways the world of teenagers has changed since you were a teen? How does this influence how you communicate and interact with teens today?

As adults, we can remember some aspects of what it was like to be a teenager; however, we must recognize that the world in which teenagers live has changed dramatically over the past several decades. Some of these changes can be considered blessings. Teenagers in the United States are exposed to a greater diversity of ethnicities than were generations before them, giving them an opportunity for deeper appreciation of others and a broader perspective on the world, the universality of the Catholic faith, as well as on the variety and the beauty of the expressions of that faith throughout the world. The internet, social media, and (for some adolescents) increasing opportunities to travel outside the United States have given young people the chance to connect with the world in ways never before available in human history.

However, a number of changes in the experience of adolescence have created significant challenges for all who minister with/to young people. For example, adolescents often experience significant tension between the most prevalent aspects of the culture of the United States and the cultural norms of their family/ethnic traditions. These points of tension may involve such

[14]"Adolescence," *Merriam-Webster's Collegiate Dictionary*. 11th ed. (Springfield, MA: Merriam-Webster, 2003).

[15]*cf.* Luke 2:41-52.

things as the importance of material wealth and possessions, the value of religious beliefs and practices, the significance of family customs, and a variety of other factors. These can cause great stress on the fabric of family life. Another issue that must be addressed is the fact that sometimes, through no fault of their own, contemporary Catholic youth are unable to articulate what they believe because they are not receiving the formation they need.[16] Studies conducted by the Pew Research Center, which take a wide variety of factors into consideration, indicate that adolescence is increasingly a time when Catholics choose to leave their faith, because they do not find it meaningful or relevant to the circumstances of their lives.[17]

The Vision of Adolescent Catechesis

What word or phrase from this vision statement speaks most powerfully to you? Why? What implication does this statement have for you and your role as a catechist?

"Young people grow in their Catholic faith by falling in love with the person and message of Jesus Christ, and mature in faith when they let that love form and transform them within the Church, a community of disciples. Adolescent catechesis is one stage of a lifelong process of embracing the Catholic way of life that forms young disciples by empowering them to know and follow Christ in their daily lives, thus becoming leaven for the Kingdom of God in the world." (National Initiative on Adolescent Catechesis, Vision and Outcomes Statement, 2009.)

This statement clearly indicates that the goal of adolescent catechesis is no different than the goal of catechesis in general: to make disciples. Furthermore, it recognizes that adolescent catechesis is a seed-sowing endeavor that we hope will lead to a lifetime of encounter, growth, and living witness within the Catholic community. Moreover, it envisions a catechesis that not only produces future disciples, but also recognizes young people as agents of transformation in the places where they currently live.

[16]Christian Smith; Melinda Lundquist Denton (2005-01-25). *Soul Searching: The Religious and Spiritual Lives of American Teenagers* (Kindle Locations 2773-2774, 4763-4765). Oxford University Press. Kindle Edition.

[17]Details can be found in the following studies: http://www.pewforum.org/search/?query=leaving%20catholicism and http://www.pewforum.org/2015/05/12/americas-changing-religious-landscape/, both conducted by: Pew Research Center, 1615 L Street, NW, Suite 800 Washington, DC 20036.

The result of this vision is a young person growing toward a mature discipleship. What does this look like? The document Vision and Outcomes of Adolescent Catechesis paints a picture of a person who:

How well do these outcomes reflect your idea of an adult disciple of Christ?

- sustains a personal relationship with Jesus Christ, supported through regular prayer, faith sharing, and scripture reading;
- shares the Good News through words and actions, through Christian stewardship, and by working for peace, justice, and human dignity;
- participates fully, consciously, actively, and regularly in the celebrations of the sacramental life of the Catholic Church;

Reflect on your parish/school community and rank each of these outcomes on a 1-10 scale (1 low / 10 high) with how well the community is doing at achieving these outcomes with young people. What are your community's strengths? weaknesses? What area(s) would be your top priority to foster?

- articulates the fundamental teachings of the Catholic faith and demonstrates a commitment to learning and growing in the faith;
- applies Catholic ethics, virtues, principles, values, and social teaching to moral decision-making, life situations, and interactions with the larger culture;
- discerns and uses her/his gifts to actively belong to and participate in the life and mission of the parish, school, and larger community;
- celebrates diversity (cultural/racial and ethnic) as a gift from God; pursuing the development of Christian communities across a variety of landscapes, as listed above, and;
- explores God's call to vocation through prayer, reflection, and discernment. (National Initiative on Adolescent Catechesis, Vision and Outcomes Statement, 2009.)

These outcomes are not independent of one another. They are interconnected. For example, full participation in the liturgy fosters a personal relationship with Christ. Knowing and being able to articulate Church teachings compels the disciple to discover and share the Good News through his or her words and actions. Discerning a vocation often comes from sharing and sharpening one's gifts by belonging to and participating in the life and mission of the Church.

When we examine the contents of the catechetical documents, we see that these outcomes are present in various forms. The outcomes of adolescent catechesis have not changed. The context in which they occur has changed. In light of this change in context, it is more important than ever before that those who minister to/with young people get to know them…their lives, their hopes, their doubts, and their dreams…as completely as possible.

A Missionary Approach to Teenagers

In order to attract young people who are only marginally engaged in the life of the Church, or not engaged at all, it is necessary that those who catechize adopt a missionary attitude. This implies a willingness to go out to where young people can be found. As stated by the youth themselves in the USCCB document, *Conclusions: First National Encounter for Hispanic Youth and Young Adult Ministry*, "[we want] the Church [to] provide us with trained pastoral leaders who are truly committed and willing to serve and leave their desks to go where we are."[18] This is the approach modeled by Jesus in the Gospels.

As you re-imagine yourself as a missionary within your community, what group(s) of young people might you be called to reach out to?

It is important to recognize that there are many young people who never participate in the life and mission of the parish community. Some of them are marginalized by their economic situation. Others have disabilities that make it difficult for them to actively participate. Teens who are of a different ethnicity than the majority of the parish community can feel that a particular faith community is not for them. Tragically, some young people are incarcerated, with no one reaching out to them. There are also a large group of non-Catholic teenagers who have no faith background and don't know what it means to be Catholic (or that they could become one). Fewer teenagers are coming to the Church, which is why it is so important that the Church goes to them. As members of the Church, we are called to become missionaries!

We must also remember that this missionary role is not limited to the adult catechists. In this situation, perhaps the most important missionaries are young people who are already involved in the catechetical program. They are called to be evangelizers and peer ministers for those who are being invited to enter into the life of the Church. It is vitally important that we train, encourage and support the adolescents in our programs who are in a position to evangelize and catechize in this way. Jesus came to "seek and save the lost."[19] We who are commissioned to pass the faith on to young people should be prepared to share the Gospel, not only with the young people

[18]National Catholic Network de Pastoral Juvenil Hispana, *Conclusions: First National Encounter for Hispanic Youth and Young Adult Ministry* (Washington, D.C.: USCCB Publishing, 2008), pg 48.

[19]Mark 10:28.

who attend our parish programs, but with those who have not yet felt the tender embrace of Christ and his Church. How we approach this mission will vary, depending upon the catechetical situation. We begin by embracing an attitude of humility such as Jesus demonstrated when he washed the feet of the disciples. As stated elsewhere in this document, it is important that the catechist show interest in things that are important to the adolescent, such as his/her cultural heritage, family background, personal interests, hobbies, and the like. It is also important to support young people as they experience significant events in their lives.

Recall a significant experience you have had with a young person. How did it come about? What was most transformative in that moment of accompaniment?

Many dramatic moments in the Gospel occurred when Jesus was on the way from one location to another and had a conversational moment that was transformative. From the Samaritan woman at the well, to Zacchaeus in the tree, to the disciples on the road to Emmaus, Jesus stopped, encountered people in the context of their lives, and invited them to accept, wholeheartedly, God's invitation to them. For those who work with young people, it is not uncommon that a conversation or occurrence outside of a formal catechetical setting can have a significant impact on both the teenager and the catechist. Though this requires extra effort on the part of the catechist, such instances often result in teenagers becoming more open to sharing their stories and more receptive to what the catechist has to share as well. This is the "extra mile" that we must be willing to walk with a teenager if we are to truly be a missionary of faith. Pope Francis mentions five actions or movements that comprise missionary discipleship: The willingness to take the first step without fear, to get involved, to provide accompaniment, to bear fruit, and to rejoice. These five actions articulated in The Joy of the Gospel (para. 24) can be of great help in forming missionary disciples.

St. Teresa of Calcutta once said, "Let no one ever come to you without leaving better and happier. Be the living expression of God's kindness: kindness in your face, kindness in your eyes, kindness in your smile."[20] In *Conclusions*, the young people clearly stated that they long for "persons who serve as role models for us and help us in our formation process."[21] When approaching teenagers we, as catechists, must be prepared to accept them for who they are and not be afraid to be challenged by their insecurities, doubts, and fears. Rather, we should seek to see their strengths, understand their personal journeys, and support their longing for God's tenderness.

[20]St. Teresa of Kolaota quoted in John Templeton, Worldwide Laws of Life: 200 Eternal Spiritual Principles (1998) p. 448.

[21]Conclusions: First National Encounter for Hispanic Youth and Young Adult Ministry, p. 48.

Creating a Strong Foundation for Adolescent Catechesis

For adolescent catechesis to be effective in our parishes and schools, five critical elements need to be in place. These elements identify and strengthen the key influences on the faith-lives of young people, widen the net of those engaged in adolescent catechesis, and call for intentional visioning and planning. All five are interconnected and fundamental to effective catechesis. They are:

- empowering parents and faith-filled families;
- creating vibrant, youth-friendly parishes;
- forming fruitful partnerships;
- engaging in comprehensive ministry to youth with intentional and systematic faith formation; and
- developing an environment of inclusion, trust, and acceptance.[22]

Empowering Faith-Filled Families

For years the Church has reminded us that one of the most important roles of parents is their role as the primary educators in the faith,[23] and research has clearly indicated that young people reflect the faith lives of their parents.[24] This is as true now as it has ever been. However, we cannot assume that the young are living in a dual parent home with both parents being Catholic. They may be living in a dual religion home, a single parent home or as a blended family with step-parents.

In addition, we must acknowledge that, increasingly in our nation, the parental role is being assumed by individuals other than the "natural" or even "adopted" parents. Many children are

[22]cf. National Initiative for Adolescent Catechesis, *Vision and Outcomes Statement,* p. 1.

[23]Congregation for the Clergy, *General Directory for Catechesis*, (Vatican City: Libreria Editrice Vaticana, 1997), no. 255.

[24]Christian Smith with Melinda Lundquist Denton, *Soul Searching: The Religious and Spiritual Lives of American Teenagers* (New York: Oxford University Press, 2005), p. 216.

raised by foster parents, grandparents, aunts and uncles, or even friends of the family. And there is another very important factor to consider: more than half of Catholics residing in the United States belong to cultural and ethnic communities that experience two different cultural realities in their every day lives and rely on the influence of the entire family when raising children/young people.

Therefore, the role of the family in catechizing youth cannot be overemphasized! It is of paramount importance that those who are responsible for adolescent catechesis at the parish and/or school must partner with parents, grandparents, legal guardians, and other family members to create a "web of influence" that will assume the important responsibility for transmitting the faith to teenagers. The Church wishes to cooperate with parents and family systems through various suitable pastoral initiatives, in order to assist them in the fulfillment of their catechetical mission.[25]

In what manner does your parish/school program currently partner with parents/grandparents/guardians in the faith transmission process? How might it be strengthened by partnering with them more intentionally within the faith formation process?

One of the best ways to find out about a teenager's family situation is to simply ask him or her to share as much as he or she feels comfortable saying. It is better to ask than to assume. This information is not gathered to label or to judge the young person. It is necessary in order to understand and respect each young person and his or her family situation so that we can better minister to him or her effectively.

In what ways can providing opportunities to engage families strengthen not only your ministry but the families themselves?

In the process of gathering the information, we will sometimes learn that there are families that don't actively participate in the faith, often because there has not yet been an opportunity to discover a relationship with Jesus Christ. The key purpose of every faith formation program is to become the facilitator of recognizing Christ within the family experience. The way we engage and encourage families helps them develop the language of the faithful through the living of their lives.

[25]Pope Francis, *Amoris Laetitia*, Apostolic Exhortation (Vatican City: Libreria Editrice Vaticana, 2016), p. 67.

Currently, many programs for adolescents suffer from a disengaged family unit. This can present itself in various ways. For example, parents may feel inadequate, or even disconnected from the Church, and thus ill-prepared to share the faith. This prompts them to leave their role as primary catechists to those who staff the parish catechetical program. This can be discouraging to all involved, but it actually does provide an opportunity for the parish to assist the family in discovering a profound experience of relationship with Jesus Christ. New models of faith formation can encourage reaching out to families, seeking to understand their stories, and journeying alongside them through patience, love, and acceptance, with the prayerful hope of discovering the presence of God's movement in their lives. This may require one parish catechist for every one or two families. In the process, it will surely challenge parishes to embrace a living discipleship. In addition, it could inspire a catechetical experience that provides constant opportunities for evangelization.

What might the parents/grandparents/guardians say if asked what role they want faith to play in their children's lives? How can the parish/school accompany them in making these hopes a reality?

As we engage such a model of catechesis, we will begin to know our young people and their families, often discovering that parents and/or other key members of the family are indeed interested in practicing their faith in the home, but are seeking assistance and support to do so. A community model can provide that support. Having a catechist work with one or two families can pose opportunities for faith sharing, prayer experiences, and the nurturing of a faith experience that families can practice together at home, in the parish, and beyond. In addition, we should encourage families to enhance these catechetical experiences by sharing cultural practices and seasonal rituals, such as celebrating Dia de Reyes (Three Kings' Day) or the Święconka (blessing of the Easter foods). Catechists can also teach and encourage new family rituals such as morning and evening prayers, grace before meals, family rosary, and the blessing of young people when they leave home each day."[26]

Also, care should be taken in forming catechists in their own faith, as well as in matching catechetical leaders to the experiences of those whom they catechize. For example, in the case of parents who are new immigrants and live in a bilingual family, encouragement and resources should be provided to stimulate a conversation about the faith that connects parents and teens across languages and generations. Or in the case of families with dual-religion homes, forming catechists in ecumenical and interfaith experiences would be recommended. And in the

[26]One resource for this is "Strong Catholic Families, Strong Catholic Youth" provided by the NFCYM, available at http://www.strongcatholicfamilies.org.

circumstance of single family homes or divorced homes, assuring catechists are formed in the theology of marriage and the annulment process would be a pastoral approach.

Families need the help of the entire faith community to strengthen their commitment to raise their children in faith. We now turn to the role of the parish, as a whole, in the process of adolescent catechesis.

Vibrant, Youth-Friendly Parishes

> *How welcoming to young people is your faith community? In what ways is it actively engaging young people in the life and mission of the parish? Where could improvement be made to help teens become more connected and included?*

It is extremely difficult to engage young people in catechesis if they are not engaged in their parish. In some cases, young people have commented that they do not always feel welcome to attend parish functions or participate in parish organizations. This can be particularly true for young people from minority ethnic groups. A critical component of the foundation for effective adolescent catechesis is to ensure that our parish communities are places where young people would like to be. A youth-friendly community of faith has the following qualities:

- joy-filled believers who truly live and celebrate their faith;
- well-planned liturgies with homilies that speak to the realities of the lives of young people;
- opportunities for teens to be clearly present and active in all aspects of parish life;
- young people who are enthusiastic and are prepared to lector and sing at liturgies, have a voice in parish leadership, and participate in various parish ministries (not just those exclusive to "youth");
- opportunities for young people with different interests, or from different ethnic communities, to engage in more than one youth group or activity;
- partnerships between parishes and Catholic schools that support each other; and
- intentional opportunities for intergenerational relationships that are beneficial to both teenagers and adults.[27]

[27]Ideas reflected in *Renewing the Vision* (modified), p. 13.

How closely does the membership of your parish community reflect the demographics of the local community? What strategies can be used to reach out to groups that may be underrepresented in the parish?

The beginnings of a parish atmosphere that is welcoming to young people are formed when a group of adults and youth together, supported by parish leadership, advocate for a greater presence for young people within the faith community. Young people need the role models and mentors who will introduce them to leadership opportunities and provide loving, supportive relationships within the context of the parish setting. Conversely, parishes benefit greatly from the vitality, enthusiasm, and creativity our young people can bring. The concept of *inclusion* is a vitally important part of this process. If our ministry to/with youth is not a ministry designed to integrate young people into the heart of the parish community, while also respecting their various racial and ethnic backgrounds, that ministry will do more to segregate them from the parish community than to integrate them. The presence of many and varied youth groups and initiatives is a gift to any parish. However, care must be exercised to assure that such groups and experiences are interconnected with the various ministers and ministries of the parish community, and are well coordinated.

Pope Francis writes, "Even if it is not always easy to approach young people, progress has been made in two areas: the awareness that the entire community is called to evangelize and educate the young, and the urgent need for the young to exercise greater leadership."[28] Teenagers must find welcome and meaningful engagement in parishes alive with rich and vibrant faith. This requires collaboration among parish leaders working together for the renewal of parish life. A critical first step is to advocate for a greater presence of young people within the faith community.

What leadership and/or additional resources are needed to help young people become more engaged in the entirety of parish life?

Finally, a youth-friendly parish also prioritizes resources and personnel for all the ministries with youth, including those of various cultural backgrounds, family structures, (dis) abilities/special needs and talents, and life experiences. Every parish should have a person who is responsible for youth ministry in the parish community. That individual should not limit the ministry to forming a youth group, but oversee and advocate for an entire parish plan that welcomes teenagers into the many aspects of parish life and comprehensively forms them in the Catholic faith. In the case of multicultural or shared parishes, where ministries are conducted in two or more different cultural contexts, this individual should also be inter-culturally competent.

[28]*Evangelii Gaudium*, no. 106.

Fruitful Partnerships

Often the approaches for catechizing adolescents are "siloed," compartmentalized among youth ministry programs, religious education sessions, school courses, families, and other ministerial entities. For adolescent catechesis to be effective, collaborative partnerships are essential. This document itself came about through a fruitful partnership of national leadership organizations representing those in youth ministry, Catholic schools, evangelization, and parish catechetical leadership. We hope it will inspire similar collaborations among many organizations and institutions that care for the welfare of teenagers.

What new or improved partnerships would help to form and transform teens into missionary disciples within the parish and the larger local community?

Intentional and mutual partnerships must be formed and nurtured among parents, parishes, dioceses, Catholic schools, apostolic movements, and adolescents working toward a common vision. Permeable boundaries[29] that allow for the sharing of resources while encouraging the seamless movement of youth between programs and ministries must be created. While the various ministries and programs may certainly have their own unique characteristics and resources, mutual enrichment and a common Catholic identity should be nurtured to strengthen a sense of ecclesial communion among all groups and initiatives, thus avoiding a culture of protective isolationism or exclusion.

A famous Ghanaian proverb which says, "It takes a village to raise a child" was adapted in *Renewing the Vision* to read, "It takes a whole church."[30] What is shared in a catechetical setting will lose its effectiveness if it is not supported, reinforced, and encouraged by the larger community of faith. These kinds of partnerships are necessary for teenagers to understand what it means to be Catholic in the world today.

How can the Catholic schools and parishes and service agencies in your local area partner to share resources and support one another's efforts in the common vision of forming missionary disciples?

Moreover, the partnerships can extend beyond the Catholic faith community. Public schools, though not focused on the faith development of teenagers, are still interested in their positive moral choices, healthy adolescent development, and growth in leadership—the same things that are a part

[29]East, Thomas, with Anne Marie Eckert, Dennis Kurtz and Brian Singer-Towns, Effective Practices for Dynamic Youth Ministry (Winona, MN, St. Mary's Press, 2004), p. 22.

[30]*Renewing the Vision*, p. 19.

of being a disciple of Jesus Christ. By engaging in such partnerships, the parish community can have a great impact in reducing the dropout rate, and can contribute to overcoming obstacles faced by young people attending public schools. It is also valuable to form relationships with local law enforcement and community social service agencies to advocate for youth at risk.[31] In summary, it is important to partner with public school administrators and counselors as well as other community leaders and organizations in order to provide additional support and assistance for teens and their families.

Comprehensive Ministry to Youth with Intentional and Systematic Faith Formation

Just as adolescent catechesis must be seen as one stage of a lifelong process, so it also must be seen as one part of a comprehensive ministry to young people that also includes advocacy, community life, evangelization, justice and service, leadership development, pastoral care, and prayer and worship.[32] Effective catechesis for young people is an important part of fulfilling the overall goals of youth ministry as stated in Renewing the Vision: to empower young people to live as disciples of Jesus Christ; to draw young people into responsible participation in the life, mission, and work of the Catholic faith community; and to foster the total personal and spiritual growth of each teenager.[33]

Catechesis is a moment within the process of evangelization,[34] the teaching and maturation stage that should follow a person's initial conversion after hearing and accepting the Gospel message (kerygma) in his or her life.[35] However, especially with adolescents, catechists must take into account that many young people have not heard a clear proclamation of the Gospel message or

[31]Gang Violence: They are Our Children. Pastoral Letter of Most Reverend Richard J. Garcia, Easter 2010.

[32]*Renewing the Vision*, p. 26.

[33]cf. *Renewing the Vision*, p. 9-17, and United States Conference of Catholic Bishops, *National Directory for Catechesis* (Washington DC: USCCB Publishing, 2005), p. 201.

[34]*Catechesi Tradendae*, no. 18.

[35]*Ibíd*, no. 20.

committed themselves to Christ.[36] This is one reason why it is so important to keep Christ at the center of catechesis. As catechists, we must realize that we are also evangelists, proclaimers of the Good News through word and deed who invite young people to be disciples of Jesus Christ.

What is your parish/school's comprehensive catechetical plan for younger and older teens? What might be missing or could be improved upon to embrace the holistic picture of Catholic faith as summarized within the four pillars?

St. John Paul II wrote that catechesis "must be systematic, not improvised but programmed to reach a precise goal."[37] This distinguishes catechesis from other forms of the ministry of the Word. Unlike initial movements of evangelization, which by their nature may be more conversational and spontaneous, catechesis should intentionally and systematically present the faith in a clear, understandable way. The Church has long embraced the "four pillar" structure for catechesis, which is described in the *Catechism of the Catholic Church*: the profession of faith, the celebration of the Paschal Mystery of Christ, living a life centered in Christ, and Christian prayer. A successful catechetical program for adolescents should help them understand:

- who God is and how God relates to us within the context of the story of salvation history, as expressed in the Creed;
- how to celebrate our faith through the liturgy and sacraments;
- what it means to live a life patterned after the teaching and example of Jesus Christ; and
- how to pray, using the Our Father as the model.

For adolescents, by virtue of their stage in life, some elements of these pillars may call for more attention than others. For example, during early adolescence, it is important to include formation on the Church's teaching regarding human sexuality. Later adolescents, looking to the future, should be helped with vocational discernment and supported along that journey. Systematic catechesis places these topics within a larger framework of understanding God's revelation and how it applies to a young person's life.[38]

It is unlikely that a teenager could get a holistic picture of the Catholic faith within one catechetical setting. This is why there must be a coordinated effort and constant communication between all of those involved with the catechesis of adolescents. If there is not a plan in place that intentionally

[36]*Ibid*, no. 19.

[37]*Ibíd*, no. 21.

[38]United States Conference of Catholic Bishops, Doctrinal Elements of a Curriculum Framework for the Development of Catechetical Materials for Young People of High School Age. (Washington, DC: USCCB, 2008), p. 1.

From your experience, what innovative approaches utilized in the formation of teens have yielded the best results? What do these approaches have in common?

leads teenagers to hear the kerygma and learn what it means to be Catholic (as expressed in the four pillars), much is left to chance.

Though catechesis is an "education in faith" it is a mistake to confine this ministry to a classroom or present it to teenagers from a purely academic point of view. While this learning style has a place in the overall catechetical formation of youth, attention must be given to the many ways teens learn and especially their need for loving mentors who can apply the Catholic faith in the concrete moments of their lives. Innovative, comprehensive learning approaches and dynamic resources must be developed along with loving, effective, and well-formed adults (young and not-so-young) willing to apprentice (acompañar) young people in the faith.

Inclusion, Trust, and Acceptance

We live in perhaps the most culturally diverse country in the world, and within it, the Catholic Church is likely the most culturally diverse community, particularly among youth and young adults. The largest group of Catholic teenagers in the United States is Hispanic/Latino, followed by non-Hispanic Whites, Blacks/African-Americans, Asians/Pacific Islanders and Native Americans. The universality of our faith and the diversity of our country provide the Catholic Church in the United States an amazing opportunity to celebrate our passion for Jesus Christ, and to continue his mission to proclaim the Reign of God in a vibrant and culturally inclusive way.

We must keep in mind that human diversity is a God-given gift uniquely embraced by the Catholic Church as a source of vitality and strength. From its very beginnings, Christianity had the universal mission to bring the Good News of Jesus Christ to every person, regardless of their social class, ability, or ethnicity. The word Catholic literally means, "universal". Such universal identity and mission, expressed so clearly in the event of Pentecost, challenged the status quo of every religion 2,000 years ago, and even today.

The multitude of cultures, ethnicities, and abilities present in the U.S. Church today must not only be acknowledged but also embraced. It is God who brings forth a rich variety of gifts, while at the same time creating a unity, which is never uniformity but a multifaceted and inviting harmony. However, in contemporary society we are witnessing and/or experiencing many forms of prejudice that tend to separate people from one another and create mistrust and fear. These include but are not limited to prejudices based on race, ethnicity, economics and disabilities; as well as the ways in which young people are often engaged by and portrayed in the media. Understanding these prejudices and working to eliminate them are essential components for a successful catechesis of adolescents in U.S. society.

Pope Francis encourages us to build bridges between people when he says: "Differences between persons and communities can sometimes prove uncomfortable, but the Holy Spirit, who is the source of that diversity, can bring forth something good from all things and turn it into an attractive means of evangelization. Diversity must always be reconciled by the help of the Holy Spirit; he alone can raise up diversity, plurality, and multiplicity, while at the same time bringing about unity." (Evangelii Gaudium, para.131.)

Who make up the various minority and/or marginalized group(s) within your faith community? Place yourself as a young person within one of those groups and step back and look at your faith community. What do you notice? Who do you identify with? Who are in leadership roles? What needs to happen differently for you to be noticed, accepted, and included for who you are?

All Catholics, particularly those entrusted with teaching the faith, should stand against unilateral separation, racial discrimination, classism, or prejudices whenever and wherever they occur; particularly in the faith community. The faith community must be a place where young people experience safety and trust, and feel at home; because it is their home. Such understanding is crucial for all of us as catechists. We must be prepared to express gestures of hospitality, closeness and joyful respect. Moreover, we must develop intercultural competency, that is: the capacity to communicate, relate, and work with people from different cultures, races, and walks of life. In addition, particular pastoral attention must be shown to young people with disabilities and those living in poverty.

Regarding catechetical ministries with adolescents from new immigrant families, it is imperative to recognize the difference between integration and assimilation. The United States Conference of Catholic Bishops states: "Through the policy of assimilation, new immigrants are forced to give up their language, culture, values, and traditions....By [ecclesial] integration we mean that all (cultural/ethnic communities) are to be welcomed to our church institutions at all levels. They are to be served in their language when possible, and their cultural values and religious traditions are to be respected. Beyond that, we must work toward mutual enrichment through interaction among all our cultures." (National Pastoral Plan for Hispanic Ministry #4)

Many of our young people (or their families) who come from different countries experience the demand to assimilate or "fit into" U.S. society. Assimilation presents an identity problem for many young people, as they feel pressured to ignore the traditions of their family and forget about their culture. After considerable research on the subject matter, Instituto Fe y Vida stresses the following:

> An individual's personal identity cannot be given by another person or be imposed from outside the individual. Parents, educators, and pastoral agents sometimes try to project their own identity onto young people…such identity substitution is not healthy for either adults or young people.[39]

Young people must be encouraged to recognize and embrace their own cultural identity as a lens through which they accept and respect the cultural identity of others. Our programs and gatherings also need to reflect the cultural realities of teens. For some communities of faith, this may mean having a variety of groupings of young people—some in different languages. In others, it may mean evaluating and adapting ministries that were initially designed for first generation young people, but must now serve second and third generation youth. When planned well—in a collaborative manner—these programs can foster unity in diversity because they reflect the common parish vision of ministry among young people.

In order to bear fruit, catechetical programs must make every effort to have people of the teens' own ethnic and cultural backgrounds in roles of leadership around them. It is vitally important for teens to see positions of faith-leadership held by people like themselves. If those leaders are

[39]Carmen María Cervantes, ed., "Evangelization of Hispanic Young People" in *Prophets of Hope, Volume 2*, (Winona: St. Mary's Press, 1995), pp. 42–43.

not currently present in the parish community, there should be an intentional effort to seek them out, train them, and fully support them.

It is vital that catechists understand the ethnic background of those whom they catechize. As mentioned previously, catechists should promote ecclesial integration rather than assimilation, and be formed to be "interculturally competent."[40] Cultural assumptions and stereotypes must be avoided, for a teenager's ethnicity does not always reflect the culture in which he or she was raised; as is the case of those who are adopted, interracial youth, and immigrants and refugees who have endured experiences in many different cultures.

Embracing diversity also includes celebrating our faith with those of other abilities, and making sure what we do is accessible to all. "Persons with disabilities...are integral members of the Christian community. All persons with disabilities have the capacity to proclaim the Gospel, offer valuable giftedness, and to serve as living witnesses to the truth of the Gospel message within the community of faith. Their involvement enriches every aspect of Church life...They [persons with disabilities] are not just the recipients of catechesis—they are also its agents."[41]

Though the overall development of every young person varies, the differences are often more pronounced in young people who have been diagnosed with an intellectual/developmental delay or impairment. The first place to look for help is from within the family. By their life circumstances, family members have become adept in understanding their loved one's disabilities. Catechists can also seek the help of trained professionals as they attempt to catechize young people with disabilities, and to assist the larger faith community as it engages people with disabilities in the life and mission of the parish.[42]

How well does your faith community embrace individuals and families with disabilities? How can your parish engage those with disabilities who are unable to regularly attend parish events and functions?

The National Directory for Catechesis states that persons with disabilities are to ...be integrated into ordinary catechetical programs as much as possible....Although providing such services is challenging to parishes and dioceses, the Church owes persons with disabilities her best efforts in order to ensure that they are able to hear the Gospel of Christ, receive the sacraments, and grow in their faith in the fullest and richest manner possible.[43]

[40]For more information on building intercultural competence visit the USCCB website: http://www.usccb.org/issues-and-action/cultural-diversity/intercultural-competencies.

[41]National Director for Catechesis, section 49.

[42]The National Catholic Partnership on Disability (NCPD) can be contacted for assistance or referrals. More information is available at http://ncpd.org.

[43]*National Directory for Catechesis*, section 49.

Young people with disabilities have a right to the same experience of community and the same quality of faith formation as youth without disabilities. Members of the faith community should have an authentic desire to know individuals' needs, aspirations and contributions in order to better experience Christ through them, and with them. Retreats, liturgies, catechetical lessons, and faith activities must be thoughtfully inclusive and reflective of a true model of accompaniment.

A challenging reality within the Church is the economic diversity of families. Unjust economic situations and the consumerism so prevalent in our culture separate the financially wealthy from the poor, and some individuals bring those distinctions into the Church. Adolescents in the United States are subject to a constant bombardment of commercials that tell them the goal of life is to own and to consume. With the insecurity that often comes in adolescence, they begin to think: "you are what you own." Those who cannot afford the latest fads, fashions, electronics, etc. can feel ashamed and excluded.

How do we help young people truly live the Gospel in relation to serving the poor and vulnerable?

Moreover, the reality that monetary wealth provides more opportunities for a successful career means that those without money have less chance of being prepared for or finding good jobs. We must challenge the reality that a growing number of adolescents are trapped in a cycle of poverty. In light of Catholic social teaching, the Church is called to be an example for solidarity and justice. We must educate ourselves and help educate others in order to become advocates for better lives for all our young people.

Those teens who are fortunate to have the necessary financial resources should be reminded of the Gospel messages of love and of justice (see: National Directory for Catechesis, pp. 173-184). It is at this young (and still formative) age that the message can have a profound impact on their hearts, helping to shape them into the moral and just leaders so desperately needed for our Church and for the world. Young people are particularly sensitive to injustices. Many catechetical programs, activities, and initiatives have a component of service to those in need. However, they should also have a missionary component that brings young people into direct contact with adolescents living on the periphery of society, through actions of solidarity and community building.

As catechists, it is imperative that we guarantee all young people have every opportunity to participate in holistic catechetical formation experiences. An environment of inclusion, trust, and acceptance must be fostered in parishes, schools, and the larger community, embracing young people and families from different cultural, ethnic, ability, and economic backgrounds. When we accept, embrace, and celebrate the diversity within the Church, we help our young people do more than just "learn" about Jesus Christ; we help them strengthen their Catholic identity, their relationship with Christ, and their commitment to be leaven for the Kingdom of God here on Earth, until Christ comes again in Glory.

Further Considerations for Adolescent Catechesis

Catechesis and Technology

Psychologist John Santrock wrote: "It has been said that adolescence begins in biology but ends in culture."[44] American teens are growing up in a different culture than the generations before them.

One of the most important aspects of contemporary culture is the profound effect of various types of media. Social media has completely altered the way young people communicate. Many adults are slow to comprehend this major shift. Media, in general, has also changed the way teens learn. They are more visual and story-driven than any previous group.

Beginning with the radio and continuing on with television, the computer, the tablet and the smart phone; media and our contemporary culture—especially as they affect our young people—have grown hand in hand. One survey of American teenagers found on average 13–18 year olds spend over nine hours a day with some kind of media.[45] This is how they entertain themselves, communicate with each other, and form their identity. We are not suggesting that media is inherently bad. It is merely a tool and, as such, can be used toward both positive and negative ends. For example, the Internet has allowed families to connect across continents; YouTube can teach new skills, and movies and books can build understanding of ourselves and others. For better and for worse, there is also a great deal of media content and message consumed by teenagers that can potentially shape the way they view themselves, others, and their faith.

How is media/technology used within your faith formation system and strategies? How much are teens empowered to develop and facilitate these strategies and models? What would young people add or change if invited to offer their ideas? How can the use of media and technology help form young people as digital disciples?

It is important to help teens identify and critically reflect on both the positive and the negative messages of media. They should not only be pointed toward positive media but encouraged to create media that shares the

[44]John W. Santrock, *Adolescence*, 8th ed. (New York: McGraw-Hall, 2001), p. 29.

[45]Common Sense Media, "The Common Sense Census: Media Use by Teens and Tweens," available at https://www.commonsensemedia.org/research/the-common-sense-census-media-use-by-tweens-and-teens.

truth of God's love with others. Doing so is one way they can be empowered to be positive change agents in their culture and in the world. Most teens already know that various forms of media can be a means for personal expression; therefore they should be encouraged to use technology as an avenue for evangelization and for sharing the values of their faith.

As today's catechists, we are called to become knowledgeable about the many technological and media tools at our fingertips. This will enable us to incorporate into our catechetical settings a variety of ways to engage youth; deepening their understanding of the faith, as well as empowering them to share their experiences of faith with others.

Declining Participation

Catholic elementary and secondary schools have a distinctive heritage of providing quality education throughout our nation. However, enrollment and tuition are two of the biggest challenges currently facing Catholic schools. Just since 2000, national Catholic school enrollment has declined by 28 percent—from 2,653,038 in 2000 to 1,915,836 in 2016, a difference of 737,202 students. (NCEA Annual Data Book, 2015 – 2016). This means that fewer students are receiving the catechesis that Catholic schools provide.

Have you personally witnessed a decline in participation by teens in your parish/school? What factors do you attribute to this? What new ideas from this document might assist and support your community in changing this trend?

By the same token, many parishes see an exodus of teenagers from catechetical programs for youth after they receive the Sacrament of Confirmation. Some parish youth ministry programs struggle to grow beyond a limited number of teenagers. In the National Study of Youth and Religion, Catholic teens fared poorly on most indicators of religiosity when compared to other Christian denominations. One of the conclusions from the survey was that:

> …many or most Catholic teenagers now pass through a Church system that has not fully come to terms with its own institutional deficit and structural vacuum with regard to providing substantial and distinctive Catholic socialization, education, and pastoral ministry for its teenagers.[46]

The challenge for all of us who are involved in adolescent catechesis on the local, diocesan, or national level is to help the Church address these issues with courage and creativity. The Epistle

[46]Smith, *Soul Searching*, p. 214.

to the Hebrews states: "For the sake of the joy set before him (Jesus) endured the cross."[47] Facing these "crosses" can be a joy when one believes that even death cannot defeat the love of God.

Allocation of Resources

To accept the challenge of strengthening and deepening the faith of young Catholics, pastoral leaders in our parishes and schools must seriously consider the allocation of resources for catechetical ministry. Though this document identifies the goals and principles for adolescent catechesis, this vision requires ministerial structures, practical strategies, and competent leadership. The vision requires an investment!

An investment in young Catholics begins with committing the time and personnel to create ministerial teams, led by catechetical and youth ministry leaders who are well formed and interculturally competent. In many parishes and schools this leadership is currently (or could be) provided by professional and credentialed lay ecclesial ministers, reflecting a significant financial investment and a commitment to just employment policies. However, many communities of faith are simply not able to provide such an investment and must therefore rely on volunteer ministry leaders who, when properly formed and trained, can be skilled at providing the vision, planning, implementation, and assessment required for a comprehensive approach to adolescent catechesis.

As a community of faith, we strengthen our commitment to young Catholics when we support the ministerial and spiritual formation of those called to minister with and to them. Whether a faith community can afford to hire a youth minister or not, it is of paramount importance that the individual who is given the responsibility for leading this ministry in the parish be properly trained and supported. As a rule, the cost of that training and ongoing formation should be assumed by the faith community.

How frequently do parish leaders and catechists take advantage of formation opportunities in their local areas, or those that are provided either within the diocese or nationally? What creative strategies might be explored to assist those who are not able to take advantage of these offerings?

We acknowledge that resources such as money, personnel, and facilities are not equally distributed across our urban, suburban, and rural faith communities. Thus we find some parishes and schools lack the qualified individuals, as well as the technology and resources necessary for effective catechetical ministry. The unique challenges and gifts

[47]Hebrews 12:2.

of these settings call for creative approaches to adolescent catechesis. Forming partnerships with parishes and organizations that can help provide the necessary resources is one way to approach this dilemma. Another potential solution involves engaging those who can assist in locating donations and grants and can navigate the application process for the necessary funds. Depending upon the circumstances you encounter in your particular setting, you might also need to create and implement other possible solutions to this challenge.

One thing is certain: research has indicated that the greater the availability of religiously based relationships, activities, programs, opportunities, and challenges for teenagers, the more likely they are to be religiously engaged and invested.[48] The allocation of resources in adolescent catechesis is of critical importance—an investment that will provide dividends for years to come.

Confirmation Preparation as an Integral Part of a Comprehensive Approach to Adolescent Catechesis

Confirmation preparation can be a significant moment for young people to encounter Christ. This happens when programs creatively, passionately, and faithfully convey what it means to be Catholic, providing teenagers with numerous opportunities to encounter loving and exemplary leaders who are willing to walk with them in their journey of faith. When intentionally integrated into a comprehensive approach to adolescent catechesis—one that includes formation leading up to and continuing after Confirmation—it can also foster a life-long relationship with the Church.

Often the approach to preparation for the Sacrament of Confirmation unintentionally fosters a mentality that Confirmation is a form of graduation. Rather than a sacrament of initiation, many young people, as well as their parents, perceive Confirmation preparation as the final piece of the formation puzzle, providing them with a convenient exit from a commitment to ongoing formation in faith. We must re-educate both young people and their parents, so that they can appreciate the value and the joy to be found in the process of lifelong faith formation…continuing to deepen our love for and devotion to the Lord, for all of our days.

How is Confirmation viewed by the majority of young people and parents in your faith community? What has contributed to this view? What changes, if any, would you propose to embrace Confirmation as a life-changing encounter with Jesus Christ?

In addition, there is a need to evaluate whether our current approaches to Confirmation preparation are effective in fostering a life of discipleship, or if they are seen as "assembly

[48]Smith, *Soul Searching*, Kindle Locations 5732-5734.

lines", meant only to advance young people through the sacraments. Parish and diocesan leadership should be open to innovative ideas that can potentially provide a life-changing encounter with Christ and the Church for the teenager throughout the preparation process. Confirmation preparation should be one experience among a number of opportunities for teenagers to grow in their Catholic faith and to learn what it means to be disciples of Jesus Christ.[49]

Catechesis on Sexuality

Adolescence is a time of sexual awareness. Sexuality (i.e. puberty, dating, etc.) will always be a major part of an adolescent's life. Therefore, it should be a major focus of adolescent catechesis. A comprehensive approach to catechesis in human sexuality should be inclusive of the Church's teachings on chastity, pornography, complementarity, gender, and identity. Amoris Laetitia reminds us:

> "Sex education should also include respect and appreciation for differences, as a way of helping the young to overcome their self-absorption and to be open and accepting of others. Beyond the understandable difficulties which individuals may experience, the young need to be helped to accept their own body as it was created, for 'thinking that we enjoy absolute power over our bodies turns, often subtly, into thinking that we enjoy absolute power over creation.... An appreciation of our body as male or female is also necessary for our own self-awareness in an encounter with others different from ourselves.' "[50]

Is a catechesis on sexuality a part of the overall faith formation process? How are parents/grandparents/guardians engaged and empowered to be active participants in this conversation?

With this in mind, it is important that our catechetical ministries engage and empower parents to have conversations of substance regarding sex and sexuality with their young people. As catechists, we must be formed to competently, confidently, and compassionately communicate the Church's teaching about sexuality to young people; and to provide techniques to accompany teenagers through their understanding of these issues. Processes and resources for assisting parish and school catechists with this very important endeavor must be continually developed, made available, and updated, as necessary. We look to archdiocesan offices as well as the appropriate national Catholic organizations and publishers to help provide leadership in this area.

[49]Michael Carotta, "The Confirmation Prep Project: Final Summary Report," (Washington, DC: PAC, 2015), p. 5.

[50]*Amoris Laetitia*, no. 285, p. 214. (Note: the quote within the quote comes from: Encyclical Letter, Laudato Si', (24 May 2015), 155.

Moving Forward in Hope

A number of significant challenges have been addressed in this document, such as: a vision of catechesis that goes beyond the classroom, the need for catechists to accompany young people in their journey of faith, the importance of centering catechesis on the kerygma, and the need for those who work with teenagers to be trained in intercultural competencies, to name a few. Other obstacles will certainly be identified by those working in various catechetical situations.

The difficulty in overcoming these obstacles might tempt one to accept things as they are and not change current practice. However, in order to resist that temptation, one need only look to places in the world where Catholicism was once vibrant but has since grown cold. There are many beautiful churches, throughout Europe and on this continent as well, that are today visited more as museums than as places of worship.

Jesus said that the Kingdom of God is like a small amount of leaven that causes the bread to rise.[51] The message of the Good News when boldly proclaimed with the power of the Holy Spirit is transformative. When catechists are joyful, passionate, and encendidos (on fire), their faith is contagious and sparks the hearts of young people. As Pope Francis has written:

> An evangelizer must never look like someone who has just come back from a funeral! Let us recover and deepen our enthusiasm, that delightful and comforting joy of evangelizing, even when it is in tears that we must sow… And may the world of our time, which is searching, sometimes with anguish, sometimes with hope, be enabled to receive the good news not from evangelizers who are dejected, discouraged, impatient, or anxious, but from ministers of the Gospel whose lives glow with fervor, who have first received the joy of Christ.[52]

[51]cf. Matthew 13:33.
[52]*Evangelii Gaudium*, no. 10.

As women and men who are deeply committed to providing quality adolescent catechesis, we must present the Catholic faith to young people in a way that is beautiful, personal, and real. Out of respect for their dignity, we cannot force the faith upon them; nor do we need to alter Church teaching in an attempt to make it more palatable for a teen to believe. Sensitive to their stage of development and inclusive of their culture, we portray the Good News in the best possible light so that teens can incorporate it into their daily lives. In the process, conversations are encouraged, questions are welcomed, and honest answers are given, even if there are answers that some young people do not want to hear. Environments for adolescent catechesis must be places of inclusion and trust where teenagers don't feel judged in any way, shape, or form. When catechizing young people we must throw out all prejudices and misconceptions of teenagers in order to reach them in a deep and meaningful way. As catechists, we must partner with families, so a teenager's education and experience of the faith can be lived and celebrated at home.

The Church has recognized that "the first victims of the spiritual and cultural crisis gripping the world are the young," and notes that "any commitment to the betterment of society finds its hopes in them."[53] Teenagers are at a vulnerable time in their lives and they need the assistance of many faithful, loving adults to help them grow strong in their Catholic faith. It is not a simple task. It requires patience, preparation, perseverance, and prayer.

It is a privilege to walk with teenagers through this incredible time in their lives, a time when they are seeing the world anew and attempting to discover their places in it. Saturated in media and surrounded by voices that pull them in every direction, effective catechesis with adolescents helps them to hear the voice of the Good Shepherd, the voice of truth, the voice of love. Those

[53] *General Directory for Catechesis*, no. 181.

who have been a part of this ministry can attest that accompanying even one young person and witnessing his/her transformation in the Holy Spirit, is worth all the challenges.

Name three things this document has inspired you and your faith community to want to do differently in helping to transform young people into missionary disciples. Who needs to be a part of this conversation before you take the next steps toward making these changes a reality? What new resources or additional training is required for your success?

Pope Francis has encouraged those in the Church to "abandon the complacent attitude that says: 'We have always done it this way.'"[54] Doing adolescent catechesis today calls for nothing less than re-imagining current faith formation and pastoral ministry efforts with young people and their families. Pastoral leaders must engage in honest assessments of current efforts and systems in order to create new relationships and patterns of ministry that work together to form disciples for Jesus Christ. Hopefully, this document will inspire conversation, encourage innovation, and result in more effective implementation of a unified vision for adolescent catechesis in the United States.

God is with us!

[54]*Evangelii Gaudium*, no. 33.